THE SECRET THOUGHTS OF
DOGS

THE SECRET THOUGHTS
OF
DOGS

BY

CJ Rose

THE
collective
BOOK STUDIO

You're switching me to dry food?

Just let them get a little farther away from the picnic basket, and then we move in.

This is your formal
invitation to
accompany me
to the dog park.

Here,
kitty kitty.

I know he said we are going to the park, but that was definitely the "we are actually going to the vet" voice.

I will catch this wingless bee if it is the last thing I do!

The hairless ape that feeds me is late again.

That is definitely the biggest cat that I have ever seen.

If this ball could throw itself, then I would only need you for the food thing.

Let's just
get this straight—
the wind knocked
this over, and I am
just helping to
clean up.

I'll give *you* potty training.

This belly is not just going to scratch itself, buster.

Just put down the
phone, get up off the
couch, and get out
here already.

No, I don't think it would be fun for your two-year-old to ride me like a horse, actually.

Why do you persist in putting me in these ridiculous contraptions?

And for my next magic trick, I shall make this kitten disappear.

Finally!
A tree that no other
dog has *ever* peed on!

I honestly can't see
a dang thing.

Best.
Pillow.
Ever.

Please, please
let tonight be
"Burger Night."

Why did I ever agree to a staring contest with this pony?

Um, that whole "taking the temperature" thing was a little awkward.

I beg of you,
please, please put
those fireworks back
in the garage cabinet.

I finally trained her to give me a treat if I shake her hand.

I *so* woke up on the wrong side of the floor today.

It's high time for you to get a life and stop dressing me in these ridiculous outfits.

I've tried them all, and this brand of toilet definitely makes the best drinking water.

I know you
think you're super
clever, but did
you really need to
name me "Spots"?

I officially
hate you.

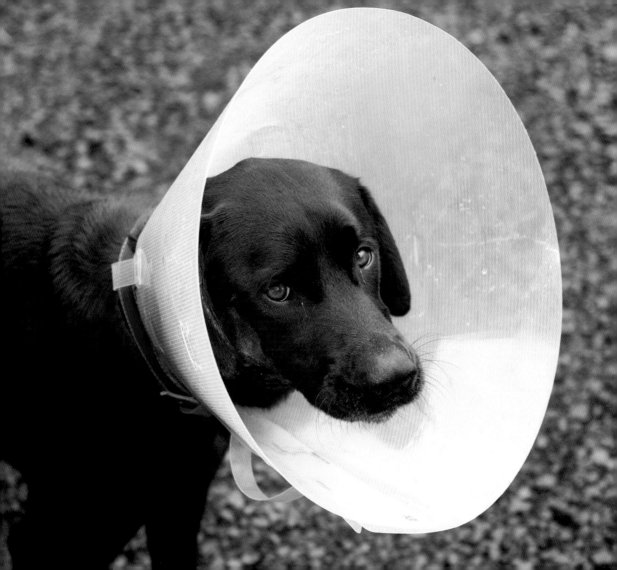

How about you sleep on the floor instead, and I just stay right here?

You realize that the second this is over I am going to go roll on a dead bird.

Know what else is fun? Peeing on the kitchen floor and watching the humans flip out.

Right after this is the pedi-pedi, then a light lunch, and "spa day" is a wrap.

Today, when you leave me all day to "bring home the bacon," can you actually bring back some bacon?

I can see that you are about to mistakenly jump to a conclusion concerning these muddy paw prints.

Oh, wait, now I
remember you.

I don't speak cat,
but I am pretty
sure that the hissing
sound means
"please chase me."

I agree, it *is* super weird looking. But let's eat it anyway.

The cat and the
human can poo inside.
But when I do,
it's like the world
has ended.

Can you throw this a hundred more times?

Yes, I'd love a meatball! That's like combining the two best things in life!

Whoever sculpted you was a genius.

Oh look, a "No dog poop, please" sign. Request denied!

Almost ready to run home and break in the new couch.

Can you drop something already?

Just a heads up that if we see my dog friends, I am going to have to act like I despise you.

Clearly I have no plans to "leave it," so you might as well stop shouting that.

Just keep pretending to look sad until he pulls away, and then let's tear this joint apart!

You are torturing me
in a desperate attempt
to look cool.

Oh, the new mailman looks delicious!

Why can't the humans stay huddled together, so I can stop worrying about herding them?

It was the cat's idea.

Incoming!

This is humiliating!
Just make a human
baby already!

It doesn't actually taste like bacon, but I still love it.

Oh, this is comfy up here. Now I know why the cat likes it so much.

This day just keeps getting better and better!

I know that I am supposed to be man's best friend, but quite honestly I prefer you.

Copyright © 2021 Steelhead Books Services, LTD.

Library of Congress catalog in Publication data is available.

ISBN 978-1-951412-22-7
LCCN 2021931853

Printed and bound in China by
Reliance Printing Company Limited, Shenzhen

Cover and interior design by AJ Hansen.
All images courtesy of Shutterstock.

10 9 8 7 6 5 4 3 2 1

Published by The Collective Book Studio
4517 Park Blvd., Oakland, CA 94602